TRULY TRULY

I Tell You the Truth

TOM CRAWFORD

WESTBOW
PRESS®
A DIVISION OF THOMAS NELSON
& ZONDERVAN

WestBow Press books may be ordered through booksellers or by contacting:

WestBow Press
A Division of Thomas Nelson & Zondervan
1663 Liberty Drive
Bloomington, IN 47403
www.westbowpress.com
1 (866) 928-1240

ISBN: 978-1-5127-1780-8 (sc)
ISBN: 978-1-5127-1781-5 (hc)
ISBN: 978-1-5127-1779-2 (e)

Library of Congress Control Number: 2015917654

Print information available on the last page.

WestBow Press rev. date: 11/19/2015

The Bible is Truth.

From Genesis to Malachi, from
creation to the Prophets, God
revealed Himself and established a
covenant with His chosen people.
This relationship allowed His
believers to learn His expectations
and to fathom His perfect judgment and
incomparable love. Prophecy
in the Old Testament told that a
Messiah would come from the
Jewish people.

Jesus Christ of Nazareth is this promised Savior. He is
God's only Son, in flesh, who came as the atonement
for mankind's sins. His arrival in the New Testament
confirms God's continued work in the earth.
In the Epistles, we learn about Jesus and the
Christian life through the inspired writings of
the Saints. In the Gospels and the Acts of the
Apostles, we are given His genealogy, birth,
life, miracles, death, resurrection,
and ascension.

We also receive His sacred lessons -
His unparalleled Word!

At times Jesus prefaced the
message He gave with *"Truly Truly"*. All
His instructions and teachings
are significant; the Beatitudes, the Lord's
Prayer, and the Parables are
all exceptional, yet the Truly Trulys
are set apart.

The one true Son of God has
emphasized these subjects, making
it clear we should examine them.
We have to pay attention!

We need to study our Bibles daily
in order to learn and grow in Christ. We should get to
know God's Word and put it to use in our lives through
Bible studies, prayer groups, and listening to sermons.

Separating, analyzing, and praying about
the Truly Trulys is one way
we can pinpoint what Jesus wants
for us in our Christian walk.

John 8:58

. . . .

Truly, Truly, I say to you, before
Abraham was born, I Am

John 8:58

. . . .

The Jewish audience Jesus was speaking
to in the temple would
have understood how complex and
powerful this statement was.

Study Exodus 3:14.

Our Christ Jesus was here before Abraham,
the original father figure
of Judaism.

What impact did this statement
have on His audience?

Matthew 11:11

. . . .

*Truly I say to you, among those born
of women there has not arisen anyone
greater than John the Baptist*

Matthew 11:11

. . . .

Study Malachi 4:5-6.

The Prophet had reported that Elijah
would appear before the Messiah.

How important is John the Baptist
in our Christian walk?

How well do we need to know him
and his message of repentance?

John 1:51

. . . .

Truly, Truly, I say to you, you will
see the heavens opened and the angels of God
ascending and descending on the Son of Man

John 1:51

. . . .

Nathanael proclaimed his faith in
Jesus upon first meeting Him.

Study Genesis 28:12-17.

Jesus was an accomplished teacher
of Jewish Scripture (some of His followers
called Him Rabbi). Here
He referenced a passage Nathanael
would have been familiar with.

Why did Jesus quote the Prophets
to teach His message?

John 5:25

. . . .

Truly, Truly, I say to you, an hour is coming and now is, when the dead will hear the voice of the Son of God, and those who hear will live

John 5:25

. . . .

Jesus healed a seriously sick man
at Bethesda. It was the Sabbath, so the
Jews were conspiring to kill Him.
Jesus used the opportunity to assert His
authority as the Son of God.

Study John 5:26-29.

The Father has given the Son the power to judge
all the dead. The saved who *hear* Him receive
the blessing of eternal life in heaven;
the lost have eternal condemnation
in hell (separated from God).

Mark 8:12

. . . .

*Truly I say to you, no sign will
be given to this generation*

Mark 8:12

. . . .

The Pharisees, a particularly sanctimonious
group of Jews who strictly observed the Law,
were demanding a sign from Jesus,
to test Him.

How did Jesus react to their test?

Are we living today in the *generation*
Jesus was speaking of?

Matthew 26:13, Mark 14:9

. . . .

Truly, Truly, I say to you, wherever
the gospel is preached in the whole
world, what this woman has done will
also be spoken of in memory of her

Matthew 26:13, Mark 14:9

. . . .

While eating at the home of Simon the leper,
a woman anointed Jesus with very expensive
perfume. Shortly after this meal, Judas Iscariot
betrayed our Lord to the chief priests.

Our good deeds in Christ's name will not
be forgotten and He will reward
us eternally.

What was the reaction of those present at the table?

Was their attitude true or hypocritical?

John 13:21, Mark 14:18,
Matthew 26:21

. . . .

Truly, Truly, I say to you that
one of you will betray Me

John 13:21, Mark 14:18,
Matthew 26:21

. . . .

Jesus knew Judas Iscariot was His betrayer. During the Last Supper He allowed Judas to leave the meal in order to go to the chief priests. The Son of God knew His time had come.

Study John 13:18.

There were many ways Christ could have gone to the cross. Why did Jesus allow Judas the betrayer into His inner circle?

John 13:38, Mark 14:30,
Matthew 26:34

. . . .

Truly I say to you that this very night, before a rooster crows, you will deny Me three times

John 13:38, Mark 14:30,
Matthew 26:34

. . . .

Jesus told Peter that he would fail
Him multiple times under pressure.
Peter, filled with the Holy Spirit,
would go on to lead the Church
as a strong and fearless
advocate of Jesus Christ.

Christ does not condemn us for our
failures, though He does demand
our repentance.

How did the Holy Spirit change
Peter after Jesus ascended?

John 16:20

. . . .

*Truly, Truly, I say to you, that you will weep
and lament, but the world will rejoice; you will
grieve, but your grief will be turned into joy*

John 16:20

. . . .

Jesus comforted and prepared the
Disciples during the Last Supper.

He used the childbirth illustration to show
the Disciples what was ahead
for them - grief during the trial and crucifixion,
then joy upon His resurrection and ascension -
as they went out to establish
the Church in His name.

Mark 14:25

. . . .

Truly I say to you, I will never again drink
of the fruit of the vine until that day when
I drink it new in the kingdom of God

Mark 14:25

. . . .

Jesus is the new wine.

Read John 2:1-11.

The first miracle of His ministry as well
as the final meal with His Disciples
both had wine as a central theme.

What is the role of wine from a
biblical perspective?

Matthew 10:23

. . . .

*Truly I say to you, you will not finish
going through the cities of Israel
until the Son of Man returns*

Matthew 10:23

. . . .

Christ empowered the Disciples to
heal sicknesses and drive out
demons, then sent them out
with detailed instructions.

Read Matthew 10:1-42.

Though He was speaking to them
specifically, we are also tasked
to be missionaries.

Study Acts 1:7-8 and Mark 16:15.

John 21:18

. . . .

*Truly, Truly, I say to you, when you were
younger, you used to gird yourself and
walk wherever you wished; but when
you grow old, you will stretch out your
hands and someone else will gird you, and
bring you where you do not wish to go*

John 21:18

· ·

Jesus was speaking to Peter, during
His third appearance to the Disciples,
prophesying the way Peter would die.

Jesus always makes it clear that the
believer's walk is not easy, that we will be
hated and persecuted, but that through the
pain we will receive a glorious reward!

Did this message prevent Peter from going
out to proclaim the Good News of Christ?

Matthew 24:2

. . . .

*Truly I say to you, not one stone of
the temple will be left upon another,
which will not be torn down*

Matthew 24:2

· ·

As the Disciples commented on
the temple's size and workmanship,
Jesus clarified to them that the
things of this world will not last, including the temple
(the greatest symbol of Judaism at that time).

We should be in awe of our Christ Jesus
who will never perish, not
man-made buildings that will
one day fall.

What message did Jesus convey in
describing the temple's destruction?

Mark 13:30, Luke 21:32,
Matthew 23:36, Matthew 24:34

. . . .

Truly I say to you, this generation will not pass
away until all these things take place

Mark 13:30, Luke 21:32,
Matthew 23:36, Matthew 24:34

· ·

The Disciples were questioning Jesus as they walked around the temple grounds. They wanted to know what signs to look for before His return.

Was Jesus describing the forty years between His resurrection and the destruction of the temple?

Should we examine these warnings in relation to modern-day events?

Matthew 19:28

. . . .

*Truly I say to you, that you who have
followed Me, in the regeneration when the
Son of Man will sit on His glorious throne,
you also shall sit upon twelve thrones,
judging the twelve tribes of Israel*

Matthew 19:28

. . . .

This is the splendid reward Jesus promised to His Disciples. Peter had asked what they were to receive after leaving everything and following Jesus.

Judas Iscariot was among the twelve
this promise was given to.

What do you think his role is now?

Matthew 5:18

. . . .

Truly I say to you, until heaven and earth pass away, not the smallest letter or stroke shall pass from the Law until all is accomplished

Matthew 5:18

. . . .

The Laws given to Abraham and Moses
are from God, perfect and eternal.

Study Romans 8:3-4.

Christ Jesus was sent by the Father
to strengthen the Law.

What is the *all* to be *accomplished?*

John 5:19

. . . .

Truly, Truly, I say to you, the Son can do nothing of Himself, unless it is something He sees the Father doing; for whatever the Father does, these things the Son also does in like manner

John 5:19

. . . .

Our Savior healed on the Sabbath at the
pool called Bethesda. The Jewish leadership,
bound by the Law, wanted to kill Jesus. This
was a portion of His response to them.

Read John 10:37-38.

In which other passages does Jesus
explain and confirm the Trinity?

John 5:24

. . . .

Truly, Truly, I say to you, he who hears My word, and believes Him who sent Me, has eternal life, and does not come into judgment, but has passed out of death into life

John 5:24

· ·

Jesus continued to reprove the Jews after the healing at Bethesda. God has given Him the power to judge both the living and the dead.

Study Romans 8:1-2.

Was the man whom Jesus had healed a witness to this exchange between the Pharisees and our Lord?

In what ways could this experience have changed him?

John 8:51

. . . .

Truly, Truly, I say to you, if anyone keeps
My word he will never see death

John 8:51

· ·

Jesus was accused by the Jews of having a demon
as He taught in the temple. He answered their
charges and added this warning for them.

Study *keeps My word.*

What are the similarities and the
differences between John 8:51
and John 6:47?

Study 1 Corinthians 15.

John 6:47

. . . .

*Truly, Truly, I say to you, he who
believes has eternal life*

John 6:47

. . . .

When our Lord told His followers
that He had come down from heaven,
they were upset because they knew His earthly family.
He then explained the importance of belief in Him.

Study John 6:44-46.

Study Isaiah 54:13.

Is there a scriptural differentiation
between faith and belief?

John 6:53

. . . .

*Truly, Truly, I say to you, unless you eat
the flesh of the Son of Man and drink His
blood, you have no life in yourselves*

John 6:53

· ·

Jesus used this graphic imagery to reveal the importance of His living sacrifice. Through Him we have vitality here and now as well as eternal life.

He is the Bread of Life.

How does the flesh of Jesus compare to the manna God provided His people in the wilderness (Exodus 16)?

John 10:1, John 10:7

. . . .

*Truly, Truly, I say to you, he who does not enter
by the door into the fold of the sheep, but climbs
up some other way, he is a thief and a robber*

*Truly, Truly, I say to you, I am
the door of the sheep*

John 10:1, John 10:7

. . . .

Shortly after upbraiding the Pharisees
for their spiritual blindness, Jesus
spoke this parable to the crowd.

Study Numbers 27:16-17.

The Good Shepherd gives His life for
His sheep. He calls them by name
and they know His voice. He goes
ahead of them and they follow.

Who are the thieves and robbers?

John 14:12

. . . .

Truly, Truly, I say to you, he who believes in Me, the works that I do, he will do also; and greater works than these he will do; because I go to the Father

John 14:12

. . . .

Jesus again substantiated His
position in the Trinity, this time to
Philip during the Last Supper.

The Disciples did not realize that Jesus
had to ascend to the right
hand of the Father, and that His departure
would allow the Holy Spirit
to reside in them. Later they would perform
the same miracles as Christ!

Study *greater works than these.*

Study John 14:16 and John 16:7.

John 16:23

. . . .

*Truly, Truly, I say to you, if you ask the Father
for anything in My name, He will give it to you*

John 16:23

. . . .

While Jesus Christ was living among
them, His Disciples had no need to ask
because He provided for them. In this
verse He gave them permission to ask
in His name once He had gone.

God is exalted when He answers our
prayers in Christ's powerful name.

It is amazing, deserving of prayer
and contemplation, that Jesus said
anything and added no exceptions.

Matthew 8:10

. . . .

*Truly I say to you, I have not found such
great faith with anyone in Israel*

Matthew 8:10

· ·

Jesus remarked to the crowd in
Capernaum, regarding the centurion
who professed his faith in Him.

Jesus goes on to say that *"the sons
of the kingdom will be cast out into
the outer darkness"* while this centurion
reclines at the banquet
table. The Lord reserved a place
of honor in heaven for a Roman
army officer.

Who are the *sons of the kingdom*?

John 13:20

. . . .

*Truly, Truly, I say to you, he who receives
whomever I send receives Me; and he who
receives Me receives Him who sent Me*

John 13:20

. . . .

This assertion, made during the Last
Supper, has several components
to study:

The Trinity: God and Son are one and the same.

The Great Commission: We must fearlessly go
out into the world to preach His message.

Mark 9:1, Luke 9:27,
Matthew 16:28

· ·

Truly I say to you, there are some of
those who are standing here who will not
taste death until they see the kingdom
of God after it has come with power

Mark 9:1, Luke 9:27,
Matthew 16:28

· ·

Jesus was speaking to His Disciples, after feeding the five thousand. This took place a week before His radiant transfiguration.

Study Mark 9:2-9.

In this remark, was Jesus referring to James, John and Peter exclusively?

Who appeared to Jesus on the mountain?

Matthew 10:42, Mark 9:41

. . . .

For whoever gives you a cup of water to drink
because of your name as followers of Christ,
Truly I say to you, he will not lose his reward

Matthew 10:42, Mark 9:41

· ·

While in Capernaum, Jesus taught
the Disciples and prepared them
for the trials to come.

Study *he will not lose his reward.*

Christ did not say one must gain his reward
through works. Instead, he will not lose the reward
already received through God's infinite grace.

. . . .

*Truly I say to you, to the extent that you
did it to one of these brothers of Mine,
even the least of them, you did it to Me*

*Truly I say to you, to the extent that
you did not do it to one of the least
of these, you did not do it to Me*

Matthew 25:40, Matthew 25:45

. . . .

In this parable, our Lord described
the judgment to come during
His triumphant return.

Jesus specified that we are to clothe
the naked, feed the hungry, give drink
to the thirsty, invite in the stranger
and visit the sick and imprisoned.

Who are His *brothers*?

What is awaiting those who did
not do as He commanded?

How is hell described in Matthew
25:41 and 25:46?

Mark 10:15, Luke 18:17,
Matthew 18:3

. . . .

Truly I say to you, unless you are
converted and become like children, you
will not enter the kingdom of heaven

Mark 10:15, Luke 18:17,
Matthew 18:3

. . . .

Think what it means to be a child:
in need of love, care, food,
clothing, shelter, discipline and instruction.
Learning to crawl, then walk, then run.

Study Matthew 18:3-4:
One must be converted, become
like a child and be humbled before
he can enter the kingdom of heaven.

Do we give humility a place in our
daily lives as followers of Christ?

Mark 10:29, Luke 18:29

. . . .

Truly I say to you, there is no one who has left house or brothers or sisters or mother or father or children or farms, for My sake and for the gospel's sake, but that he will receive a hundred times as much now in the present age, houses and brothers and sisters and mothers and children and farms, along with persecutions; and in the age to come, eternal life

Mark 10:29, Luke 18:29

. . . .

The Disciples were jockeying for position in what they believed to be a new government with Jesus in charge. Here He responded to Peter's concerns.

Study the emphasis on *for My sake and for the gospel's sake.*

It is a beautiful promise of fulfillment now and forever, yet Jesus makes it clear that the believers' walk is not going to be easy, that there will be *persecutions.*

Are we conscious there will be *persecutions* in our walk with the Lord?

Mark 12:43, Luke 21:3

. . . .

*Truly I say to you, this poor widow put
in more than all the contributors to the
treasury; for they all put in out of their
surplus, but she, out of her poverty, put
in all she owned, all she had to live on*

Mark 12:43, Luke 21:3

· ·

Jesus was watching the rich put large
amounts into the treasury. Then a poor
widow put in two copper coins.

Study the comparison between
giving out of surplus, works,
pride, or hypocrisy and giving out
of love, faith, or fear.

Beyond tithing, is this a lesson about
giving ourselves fully (body, mind,
soul, possessions) to the Lord?

Mark 11:23, Matthew 21:21,
Matthew 17:20

. . . .

Truly I say to you, if you have faith the size of
a mustard seed, you will say to this mountain,
'Move from here to there', and it will move;
and nothing will be impossible to you

Mark 11:23, Matthew 21:21,
Matthew 17:20

. . . .

As they passed by the fig tree Jesus
had withered, He gave the Disciples
this remarkable testament to true
faith in the Lord's power and His
willingness to work through us.

Much like John 16:23, this statement
seems unattainable, so we must approach
it with added reflection and prayer.

What does it take for us to move
mountains through our faith?

Luke 12:43, Matthew 24:46

. . . .

*Blessed is that slave whom his master finds so
doing when he comes. Truly I say to you that he
will put him in charge of all his possessions*

Luke 12:43, Matthew 24:46

. . . .

Jesus made a comparison (and a warning)
between His return and a master who leaves a
slave to handle the business while he is gone.

Study Luke 12:47-48.

Who has been *given much*?

According to Matthew 24, what
will happen to the slave who is not
prepared when his master returns?

Matthew 6:2, Matthew 6:5,
Matthew 6:16

. . . .

Truly I say to you, hypocrites
have their reward in full

Matthew 6:2, Matthew 6:5,
Matthew 6:16

. . . .

Matthew 6 records a portion of
the Sermon on the Mount.

'Hypocrite' is taken from the
Greek word for 'actor'.

Jesus specifically warned against
hypocrisy when praying, fasting
and when giving to the poor.

Why did our Savior save His
harshest denouncements for
hypocrites and false teachers?

John 3:3

....

*Truly, Truly, I say to you, unless one is born
again he cannot see the kingdom of God*

John 3:3

. . . .

Nicodemus, a Pharisee, came to
Jesus secretly with many questions. Here,
Jesus described conversion,
or new birth.

Conversion comes from from the
Greek word for 'again' or
'from above', as well as the Latin
for 'turned around'.

What are the characteristic manifestations
of being born again?

John 3:5

. . . .

Truly, Truly, I say to you, unless one is born of water and the Spirit he cannot enter into the kingdom of God

John 3:5

. . . .

Our Lord continued to impress upon
Nicodemus the process of new birth.

What does birth by means of water
and of the Spirit mean?

How does the Holy Spirit work
in conversion?

John 3:11

....

Truly, Truly, I say to you, we speak
of what we know and testify of
what we have seen, and you do
not accept our testimony

John 3:11

. . . .

Jesus continued teaching Nicodemus.
As Pharisees were powerful, legalistic
experts of Judaism, Nicodemus
needed Jesus' stern correction.

True faith in Christ comes from the
heart, trusting in His Word, not from
knowing and keeping the Law.

Did Nicodemus come to know
Jesus as Lord and Savior?

John 6:26

. . . .

*Truly, Truly, I say to you, you seek Me,
not because you saw signs, but because
you ate of the loaves and were filled*

John 6:26

· ·

The crowds followed Jesus to Capernaum after
He had miraculously fed the five thousand.

He knew they were not looking for the
signs He was the Messiah, but that they
were fulfilling more base desires.

Must we experience miracles to have
faith that Jesus is our Savior?

How can we be satisfied in Christ?

John 6:32

. . . .

*Truly, Truly, I say to you, it is not Moses
who has given you the bread out of
heaven, but it is My Father who gives
you the true bread out of heaven*

John 6:32

. . . .

In Capernaum, Jesus continued to
explain to the crowds how they could
be strengthened through Him.

The original life-sustaining gift from
God to Moses' people was manna.

Study John 6:33-35.

Jesus' body and blood are the true
bread and wine of salvation.

Did the gathered crowd understand and appreciate
this truth the Savior revealed to them?

John 8:34

. . . .

Truly, Truly, I say to you, everyone who
commits sin is the slave of sin

John 8:34

. . . .

The newly converted Jewish believers had
never been enslaved by a foreign power and
were confused about Jesus' teachings.

We are either a slave to God and His holy Word
or a slave to sin and the world. The only way out
of sin is through bondage to Jesus Christ.

How often do we think of sin
as enslavement?

John 12:24

. . . .

*Truly, Truly, I say to you, unless a grain of
wheat falls into the earth and dies, it remains
alone; but if it dies it bears much fruit*

John 12:24

. . . .

In this simple illustration, Jesus showed how
after His death, resurrection and ascension,
the Church would grow exponentially.

We must die to self in order to truly
follow and know Christ Jesus, whereupon
the Holy Spirit guides us to produce
good fruit for the kingdom.

Study Romans 6 and Philippians 1:21.

John 13:16

· ·

*Truly, Truly, I say to you, a slave
is not greater than his master, nor is one
who is sent greater than the
one who sent him*

John 13:16

Our Savior spoke these words after
washing His Disciples' feet, an act
which was considered slaves' work.

The King of kings and the Lord
of lords humbled Himself and
washed His followers' feet!

What did He teach us about
having a servant's heart?

Mark 3:28

. . . .

*Truly I say to you, all sins shall be forgiven
the sons of men, and whatever blasphemies
they utter; but whoever blasphemes against
the Holy Spirit never has forgiveness,
but is guilty of an eternal sin*

Mark 3:28

· ·

This was a warning to the scribes who
accused Jesus of being demonic.

Slandering the Holy Spirit is among the
most punishable sins according to
the Son of God!

Does this strengthen or diminish the
Law as stated in Exodus 20:7?

Luke 4:24

. . . .

*Truly I say to you, no prophet is
welcome in his hometown*

Luke 4:24

. . . .

Jesus was admired and respected in His
hometown of Nazareth where they knew
His family. He taught with authority in their
synagogues, yet this day they were prepared
to throw Him off a cliff to His death.

Study Luke 4:16-30.

What did Jesus say that incited
the townspeople to riot?

Luke 12:37

. . . .

*Blessed are those slaves whom the master
will find on the alert when he comes; Truly
I say to you, that he will gird himself to
serve, and have them recline at the table,
and will come up and wait on them*

Luke 12:37

· ·

There are many instances where
our Savior warned us to be vigilant,
ready for His magnificent return.

Study Luke 12:35 and Matthew 24:42.

We are to be prepared to serve Him
as King upon His return. What is
different about this verse that He will
instead serve those He finds alert?

Matthew 5:26

. . . .

Truly I say to you, you will not come out
of there until you have paid up
the last cent

Matthew 5:26

. . . .

Jesus was expounding on several
of the Ten Commandments and
giving them a greater meaning.

Study Matthew 5:17-48.

What does this passage teach us
about forgiveness? Paying debts?
Loving our enemies? Judgment?

Matthew 10:15

. . . .

*Truly I say to you, it will be more tolerable
for the land of Sodom and Gomorrah in
the day of judgment than for that city*

Matthew 10:15

. . . .

Jesus prepared the Disciples for ministry.
When a house or city was accepting
of Christ, they were to give it their
blessing. If not, they were to shake the
dust from their feet as they departed.

Study Genesis 19:24-25 and
Luke 10:10.

Some will not accept Christ, and the
punishment for their unbelief will
be tremendous.

What happened to Sodom and Gomorrah?

Matthew 13:17

. . . .

*Truly I say to you that many prophets
and righteous men desired to see what
you see and did not see it, and to hear
what you hear, and did not hear it*

Matthew 13:17

. . . .

Jesus explained to the twelve Disciples why
He used parables to teach His message.

Study Isaiah 6:9-10.

Stubborn people, including those locked
in the Law, will not listen with their
hearts nor will they understand.

Where does our heart need to be in order
to gain Biblical wisdom and discernment?

Matthew 18:18

· ·

*Truly I say to you, whatever you bind
on earth shall have been bound in
heaven; and whatever you loose on earth
shall have been loosed in heaven*

Matthew 18:18

. . . .

Jesus taught the Disciples lessons on Church
discipline and corporate prayer.

Admonishing a sinning brother according to
Jesus' directions will carry God's approval.

Study 1 Timothy 5:19-21.

How well do we comply with the
instructions Jesus taught us in
Matthew 18:15 through 18:20?

Matthew 19:23

. . . .

Truly I say to you, it is hard for a rich man
to enter the kingdom of heaven

Matthew 19:23

. . . .

Jesus didn't say "impossible" here.
He simply wants our complete devotion.

A rich person could be more tempted,
more proud, or more distracted
than someone of lesser means.

How did Jesus view money? Taxes?
Gaining wealth? Tithing?

Matthew 21:31

. . . .

Truly I say to you that the tax
collectors and prostitutes will get into
the kingdom of God before you

Matthew 21:31

. . . .

Nearing the end of His ministry, Jesus
chastised the chief priests, ensuring
His eventual arrest and crucifixion.

Study the exchange in
Matthew 21:23-46.

A centurion, tax collectors, and prostitutes who
embrace Christ are welcome into heaven before
the hypocrites with hardened hearts.

In the Parable of Two Sons,
who are the sons representing?

Matthew 25:12

. . . .

Truly I say to you, I do not know you

Matthew 25:12

. . . .

The parable of the Ten Bridesmaids,
a message to be prudent, alert,
and prepared for His arrival.

Study Matthew 25 leading to this
frightening proclamation.

What can be the substitute for
lamp oil in our daily lives?

Matthew 18:13

. . . .

Truly I say to you, he rejoices over it more than
over the ninety-nine which have not gone astray

Matthew 18:13

. . . .

Study Matthew 18:10-14.

In Matthew's Gospel, the message is that children's angels are close to God and that He does not want even one little one to perish.

Study Luke 15:4-7.

In Luke's account, the message is repentant sinners. There is joy in heaven when we repent and return again to our Lord Jesus.

Notes and Thoughts

There are different translations of the Holy Bible, and each has a unique take on Truly Truly. The King James version is *"Verily I say unto thee"*. The Holman Christian Standard is *"I assure you"*. The New Century Version goes *"I tell you the truth"* while the New American Standard is *"Truly Truly"*.

There are nearly seventy-five messages which Jesus prefaced with Truly Truly. The audiences for these varied, with the Disciples receiving forty-two of them. Jewish audiences received eight, while mixed crowds got seven. Peter received six Truly Trulys, Nicodemus and Jewish believers each received three. Rounding out the audiences are Nathanael, Andrew, Philip, scribes, Pharisees, chief priests and a centurion.

The Disciples are the overwhelming majority of those who received the Truly Trulys. Though they had given up their "normal" lives to be dedicated followers of Jesus, they received some of His most honest reprimands (John 13:21, Mark 14:30). As He sent them out to minister in His name, Jesus never sugarcoated what to expect (John 21:18, John 16:20). Their rewards, on the other hand, are unfathomable (Matthew 16:28, Matthew 19:28).

Jesus never disparaged the customs nor history of the Jews. He is a descendant of David. Jesus is the Christ, the promised Jewish Messiah! During His lessons, He referenced Moses (John 6:32), Abraham (John 8:58), the temple (Matthew 24:2), the Law (Matthew 5:18) and other important Jewish traditions.

How can today's believers learn from these seemingly Jewish topics?

Subjects discussed within the Truly
Trulys include:

The Holy Trinity
The role of the Holy Spirit
Eternal Life
Faith in Jesus
The power in His name
The body and blood of Jesus
His authority
The Christian walk
Complete surrender to Christ
Sin
Hell
Hypocrites
Prayer
Belief
Jesus' return
Preparedness
Redemption
Forgiveness

Are other subjects covered by the Truly Trulys?

Which themes stand out most prominently?

Additional Study

Personal Notes

About the Author

Tom Crawford has been writing for all of his adult life. After coming to follow Christ Jesus at First Baptist Church of Naples, Florida, he began to examine his essays in terms of the Christian walk. Now a member of World Outreach Church in Murfreesboro, Tennessee, his passions for prayer and fellowship have grown to new and amazing heights.

Always a people person, Tom is continually raising up the men and women God puts in his path. He has been led to use his strength in the written word and couple it with his love for Christ to open up ideas for others to study.

Tom is married and has three wonderful children.

Printed in the United States
By Bookmasters